Pocket Edition 100 FACTS

Big Cats

Pocket Edition 100 FACTS

Big Cats

Camilla de la Bédoyère
Consultant: Steve Parker

Miles Kelly

First published in 2005 by Miles Kelly Publishing Ltd
Harding's Barn, Bardfield End Green, Thaxted, Essex, CM6 3PX, UK

This edition updated 2018, published 2019

2 4 6 8 10 9 7 5 3 1

Publishing Director Belinda Gallagher
Creative Director Jo Cowan
Editorial Director Rosie Neave
Cover Designer and Designer Rob Hale
Image Manager Liberty Newton
Indexer Jane Parker
Production Elizabeth Collins, Jennifer Brunwin-Jones
Reprographics Stephan Davis, Callum Ratcliffe-Bingham
Assets Lorraine King

ISBN 978-1-78617-650-9

Printed in China

British Library Cataloguing-in-Publication Data
A catalogue record for this book is available from the British Library

ACKNOWLEDGEMENTS
The publishers would like to thank the following sources for the use of their photographs:
(t = top, b = bottom, l = left, r = right, m = main)
Cover (front) Tambako the Jaguar/Getty
Deposit Photos 11(t) Andaman; 14 kyslynskyy **FLPA** 12–13(m) Jami Tarris/Minden Pictures; 15(b) Christian Heinrich/
Imagebroker; 17(r) Frans Lanting; 37(b) Patrick Fagot; 41(br) Alain Compost/Biosphoto **Fotolia** 10(tl and rt) Alexey
Khromushin **iStock** 46(m) iStock **NPL** 28(cl) and (cr) Klein & Hubert; 33(m) Vladimir Medvedev; 47(t) Roland Seitre
Shutterstock 2–3 Braam Collins; 5(tl) and 8 Nataliia Melnychuk; 5(b) and 33(t) Michael Wick; 6–7 Karen Kane – Alberta,
Canada; 9(l) Mikadun; 10(tr) Dennis W Donohue, (l) Andre Dib; 11(c) EcoPrint, (b) EcoPrint; 15(t) Hedrus; 16 Mogens
Trolle; 17(l) Nolte Lourens; 18(b) Stuart G Porter; 19(tl) Ryan M. Bolton, (r) Alan Jeffery; 20–21(m) Oleg Znamenskiy;
20(bl) Bryan Busovicki; 22(t) Larsek; 23(t) Dr Ajay Kumar Singh; 24(t) By Braam Collins; 26 milosk50; 27(t) Daniel
Dunca, (b) Jan_Broz; 28(b) Stuart G Porter; 29(m) Boleslaw Kubica, (r) Gerrit_de_Vries; 30–31 Dennis W Donohue;
34–35(m) Rich Carey; 35(br) Utopia_88; 36 Kris Wiktor; 37(t) Vadim Petrakov; 38(t) EcoPrint, (b) Kshitij30; 39(t) Villiers
Steyn; 39(inset, l) Magnus Haese; 39(b) S.R. Maglione; 39(inset, b) ecoventurestravel; 40–41(m) Martin Prochazkacz;
41(r) Ewan Chesser; 44 Dr Ajay Kumar Singh; 45(tr) elitravo, (cl) Canon Boy; 47(b) Ana Gram **Superstock** 42–43(m)

All other images from the Miles Kelly Archives

Every effort has been made to acknowledge the source and copyright holder of each picture.
Miles Kelly Publishing apologizes for any unintentional errors or omissions.

Made with paper from a sustainable forest

www.mileskelly.net

Contents

Cats – cute or killers?

1 **All cats, big and small, are killers.** Their bodies are perfectly designed to find, chase and kill animals. Unlike other hunters, such as dogs and bears, cats only eat meat. They are the supreme predators of the animal world and are amongst the most intelligent, beautiful, graceful and athletic of all creatures on our planet. While small cats have found a place in our hearts and our homes, big cats are trying to survive in a world that is taking away the space and freedom they need.

◄ The snow leopard roams a mountainous area of Central Asia where the weather is cold and few plants grow. It is quite different to other leopards — smaller and with a paler, thicker coat.

Big, bigger, biggest!

2 All members of the cat family are mammals. They are strong but swift and most can climb trees easily. Their faces are rounded and their muzzles short. Cats are predators, which means that they hunt other animals and their teeth are suitable for catching, killing and eating their prey. All cats have excellent eyesight.

◀ The Siberian tiger is covered with thick fur that keeps it warm during the winter months.

3 The tiger is not only the biggest cat, it is also one of the largest carnivores (meat eaters) living on land. Of all tigers, Siberian tigers are the biggest. They may weigh as much as 350 kilograms and can measure 3 metres in length.

MAKE A MODEL CAT

You will need:
2 cups plain flour   1 cup salt   bowl
1 cup water   varnish or paint   spoon

1. Mix flour and salt in a bowl.
2. Add water slowly, mixing as you go, Stop adding when it reaches a dough-like consistency.
3. Mould your dough into a cat shape and place on a greased baking tray
4. Bake at gas mark 1 or 120°C for one to three hours.
5. Once cool, paint or varnish your model.

4 **Jaguars are the biggest cats in the Americas.** They measure up to 2.7 metres in length and can weigh an impressive 158 kilograms, which makes them the third largest big cat.

▼ *Smilodon* probably used its huge teeth to stab thick-skinned animals.

▲ A jaguar's spots look like rosettes and often have a dark smudge in the centre.

5 **Lions hunt in groups called prides.** This means that they can catch much larger animals than big cats that hunt alone. By hunting together all the lions in the group eat regularly. Male lions usually eat first, although the females do most of the hunting. All lions spend a lot of time sleeping!

6 **The nimble cheetah does not need to be big to be successful.** It has developed into one of the world's greatest predators, proving that skill and speed can make up for a lack of bulky muscles.

7 **Sabre-toothed cats became extinct (died out) about 10,000 years ago.** The most famous was the lion-sized *Smilodon*, the canine teeth of which were a massive 25 centimetres long!

Where in the world?

8 Big cats are found mainly in Africa, Eurasia and the Americas. The place where an animal lives is called its habitat. Most big cats live in hot places where there are plenty of animals for them to hunt, but their habitats range from sun-baked deserts to snowy forests.

▶ There are about 37 species (types) of cat found in the world today. Most are solitary forest-dwellers.

▼ Pumas are found from the southernmost tip of Argentina, all the way north to Canada.

NORTH AMERICA

▲ The thick vegetation of the Amazon rainforest in Brazil offers jaguars protection from hunters.

SOUTH AMERICA

9 The Americas are home to jaguars, margays, ocelots and pumas. While some jaguars are found in Central America, they have the best chance of surviving in the Amazon basin of Brazil. Pumas can live further north and south than any other species of large land mammal on Earth.

▲ Lions live in Africa. A small number, called Asiatic lions, survive in the Gir Forest of southern Asia.

▲ Tigers live in small regions of southern and eastern Asia. Their habitats range from tropical forests to Siberian woods.

EUROPE

ASIA

10 The mighty tiger once roamed from south and Southeast Asia, all the way to the Russian Far East. Now it only survives in little pockets of land in these areas. Tigers have lost their habitat to humans who want to farm and live on the land that was once ruled by these huge animals.

▼ Cheetahs live in Africa and western Asia. Their habitat is open grasslands.

AFRICA

11 Millions of years ago the Americas were joined to Europe, Africa and Asia. The ancestors of modern cats were able to move across this huge landmass. But Australia, New Zealand and New Guinea separated from the other continents before cats appeared. That is why no cats are native to these places.

OCEANIA

▼ Leopards are found throughout Africa and Asia, in many different habitats.

12 African big cats include cheetahs, lions and leopards. Lions live on the savannah (vast grasslands). Their pale fur blends perfectly with the dry grasses of the open plains. Cheetahs also hunt on the savannah, but tend to do so during the day, when other big cats are resting.

King of the jungle

13 The tiger is the largest cat – and also one of the hardest to find. They live deep in the jungle where huge trees block sunlight, helping them to blend into the murky darkness. Their stripes camouflage them as they stalk silently through the dappled shadows, or long grass.

14 Tigers hunt by stealth, creeping up on their prey in the dark of night. They may travel several kilometres each night, roaming along tracks in search of victims. Tigers hunt for deer, wild pigs, cattle, monkeys and reptiles. They will even kill young elephants or rhinoceroses.

▶ Lions are often incorrectly referred to as 'Kings of the jungle', but it is tigers that are at home in this environment. Tigers are endangered, so if we do not do enough to save them, they may soon become extinct.

15 Tigers love to swim. When it is hot they may take a dip in lakes and rivers to cool down. They are good swimmers and can make their way across large stretches of water.

16 Although they are powerful hunters, tigers may have to stalk 20 animals before they manage to catch just one. They normally kill once every five to six days and eat up to 40 kilograms of meat in one go! Tigers often return to a kill for several days until they have finished it, or scavengers (animals that eat food left by other animals) have carried it away.

QUIZ

1. Why do tigers have stripes?
2. What name is given to animals that eat the leftovers of other animals?
3. Are tigers good at swimming?

Answers:
1. A stripy coat helps camouflage them in the forest 2. Scavengers 3. Yes

17

Bengal tigers have a reputation as 'man-eaters'. Tigers don't usually eat people unless they are too sick or old to find other prey, but some tigers prefer the taste of human flesh. Between 1956 and 1983, more than 1500 people were killed by tigers in one region alone.

18

No two tigers have the same pattern of stripes. White tigers with black stripes are occasionally seen in the wild and are bred in zoos because they are popular with visitors. Although they don't look like their parents, these tigers are not different in any other way.

Jaws and claws

◀ Long, sharp teeth paired with a bite force powered by strong jaws and neck muscles can kill a prey animal with one swift bite.

19 An animal's teeth are suited to the types of food it eats. Cats have long, sharp front teeth to bite and kill their prey. Their strong back teeth tear and chew pieces of meat.

20 Catching, killing and eating other animals is a tough job. In order to be successful hunters, cats need to have special teeth. Their pointy teeth are called canines. These are especially good for killing or holding onto prey. Behind the canines are carnassials. These teeth are ultra-sharp and they work like a pair of scissors to slice up flesh.

21 A cat's tongue is **very rough!** This is because it is covered in hard spikes, or papillae. The scratchy surface is ideal for scraping meat off bones.

◀ Cats such as these lions can make their tongues into a scoop shape, which means that they can take big gulps of water when they are thirsty.

22 The paws of big cats and **pet cats are very similar.** All cats have paws that are armed with sharp, deadly daggers – claws. The bottom surface of each paw has soft pads that are surrounded by tufty fur to muffle the sound of every footstep.

▶ Each claw on this lynx's paw is curved and very sharp – a perfect tool for digging into its prey.

Going solo

23 **Most cats are loners.** Each animal has its own patch of ground, or territory, which it lives in and defends. Cubs usually stay with their mother until they are between one and three years old. Then they have to look out for themselves. Lions, however, normally live in groups called prides.

▶ This cheetah is sniffing to find out if another cat has left a scent marking in its territory.

24 **Lions live together – and no one knows why.** It may be easier to hunt on open grasslands as a group. It's also hard to hide your supper from scavengers, such as hyenas, when there are few bushes and trees, so maybe a group of lions can send a pack of nosy hyenas on their way more easily than a single lion.

25 Cats mark their territory with their scent, which tells other cats to stay away. They do this by spraying urine on trees and bushes around their area. If a cat enters another's territory there may be a fight. Usually, big cats roar at intruders to scare them away rather than fight.

▼ Cats patrol their territories regularly. This Jaguar is sniffing a tree to check that its scent is still strong.

▼ By licking a paw to clean its face, this tiger transfers scent from glands in its chin onto its paws. It can then mark its territory as it walks.

26 Cats' fur also carries a strong scent. The scent is made by special body parts called glands. When cats wash they spread this smell all over their bodies, and as they rub against trees, the smell comes off. This is another way of marking their territory. Pet cats rub themselves against your legs to make it clear to other cats that you belong to them!

Spotted sprinter

27 A cheetah can run as fast as a car. Within 2 seconds of starting a chase, a cheetah can reach speeds of 75 kilometres an hour, and soon reaches a top speed of about 105 kilometres an hour – making it the world's fastest land animal. Cheetahs tire after about 30 seconds, so if its prey keeps out of reach for this amount of time, it may escape capture.

◀ A cheetah's body is perfectly adapted for sprinting. When it runs, only one paw will touch the ground at any one time.

28 This big cat lives in the grasslands and deserts of Africa and Middle East and Western Asia. Cheetahs do not often climb trees, as they have difficulty in getting down again. Cubs often hide in bushes so that they can surprise their prey. The word 'cheetah' means 'spotted wind' – the perfect name for this speedy sprinter.

▼ Cheetahs prefer wide open spaces where they can easily spot prey such as gazelles.

29 Like most of the big cats, cheetahs often live alone. Females live in an area called their 'home range', only leaving if food is scarce. When cubs leave their mothers they often stay together in small groups. Eventually the females go off to find their own home ranges, but the cubs may stay together and attack other cheetahs that come too close.

▼ Cheetahs kill antelopes by biting their throats, stopping them from getting any air.

30 A cheetah must rest before eating, or risk becoming dangerously over-heated. Cheetahs can spend a whole day eating if they go undisturbed by vultures or lions, which will steal the food if they can.

31 Cubs have thick tufts of long, pale fur on their heads, necks and shoulders. No one knows why – it might help to make them look bigger and stronger than they really are.

▶ Mothers keep their cubs hidden until they are old enough to start learning how to hunt.

32 There are usually between four and six cubs in one litter. Sadly, only one cub in every 20 lives to be an adult cheetah. The others are usually killed by lions or hyenas.

Home on the range

33 Thousands of years ago, nearly half of Earth's land was covered in grasslands. Since then much of it has been built upon or turned into farmland. This has contributed to the falling numbers of big cats in these areas. Some grasslands are now protected. These places have become sanctuaries for wildlife.

34 Savannahs (grasslands) occur in places where there is just enough rain to stop the land turning into desert. They are home to some of the most famous big cats. There are two seasons: wet and dry. When it rains in the wet season, the waterholes fill and the grass grows green. During the dry season, the grass is scorched to the colour of sand and big cats struggle to find enough water and food to survive.

▼ A big cat will watch a herd of grazers, like these Thomson's gazelles, for some time before making its move. If it can spot an animal that looks small, weak or old the cat will try to separate this animal from the rest of the herd, as it will be easier to kill.

▲ Anthills provide a handy lookout platform for cheetahs, so they can scan the savannah for potential prey.

35 Grass is the favourite food of animals that graze. Animals such as giraffes, antelope, wildebeest and zebra nibble at the grass, or pick leaves off the bushes and trees that litter the plain.

36 Grazing animals make a tasty meal for lions and cheetahs. With few trees to hide behind, it is difficult for big cats to surprise their prey. Cheetahs rely on speed to catch other animals, while lions hunt in a group.

I DON'T BELIEVE IT!

Many cheetahs have been killed for their beautiful fur. There are now only 12,000 left in Africa, and no more than 200 in Western Asia.

Cub class

37 **Cubs are born helpless and blind.** A group of cubs is called a litter and there are usually between two and four in each one. Cubs depend on their mother's milk for the first few months of life, but gradually their mother will introduce them to titbits of meat that she brings back to the den.

▲ Helpless newborn cheetah cubs are nursed by their mother in a rocky den or grassy lair.

▶ Mother cats such as this puma need to stay alert and on the lookout for danger. Their cubs, or kittens, make an easy target for other predators.

▶ By playing like this, these lion cubs are learning hunting skills.

38
Male lions help to look after their young. When the lionesses are hunting, the males protect the cubs and play with them. When a hunt is successful the males eat before the females, but often let the cubs eat first. All lions have black tufts of fur on the ends of their tails. The tufts don't seem to have any use except as playthings for lion cubs!

39
The babies of some cats, such as pumas, are called kittens. Adult pumas are sand-coloured, to provide them with camouflage in the deserts and mountains where they live. Their kittens are born with spots on their fur that gradually fade. Spots are better camouflage for these youngsters, which hide in bushes and undergrowth.

40
Cubs learn how to hunt from watching their mothers. Many mother cats teach their babies how to hunt by bringing them small animals that they have captured alive. When they let the animal loose, the cubs or kittens can play with it and practise their hunting skills. It may seem cruel, but it is important that the cubs learn how to look after themselves.

Cubs have a tough time making it to adulthood. Cubs are hidden by their mothers, partly to avoid bumping into any males. Male cats such as tigers kill any cubs that aren't their own.

Sociable simba

▲ Lionesses prepare an ambush by spreading out and circling their prey.

41 **Lions are sociable animals.** They live in family groups called prides that normally include between four and six adults, all related, and their cubs. Large prides of perhaps 30 animals develop where there is plenty of food.

43 **The best time to hunt is early morning or evening.** Lions hunt zebra, wildebeest, impala and buffalo. A group of lionesses has been known to bring down an adult giraffe that was 6 metres tall!

42 **Unlike other big cats, male and female lions look very different.** They both have sandy-coloured fur that blends into sun-scorched grasslands, but the males have manes of darker hair on their heads and shoulders that make them look powerful and threatening.

► Lionesses give birth to a litter of between one and six cubs. The cubs stay with their mother for over two years.

44 Although it is unusual, lions do sometimes attack and eat humans. In the 1930s and 1940s, a family of lions in Tanzania preferred human flesh to the normal lion diet of antelope. They killed nearly 1500 people in just 15 years.

45 Adult males only stay with their pride for a few years at a time. If a male wants to become the leader of another pride, it must fight the males and kill the cubs. This seems very cruel, but it does this to make the lionesses ready to have more cubs before it mates with them. The new leader then knows that all the cubs in the pride will be his own.

46 Few animals would dare to attack a healthy lion. When a lion has become old and weak, however, it may be easy prey for a band of hyenas. It is said that lions only fear hyenas – this is because they know they could end up in the bellies of several of them!

I DON'T BELIEVE IT!
Every cat's favourite pastime is napping. Lions spend almost 80 percent of their time sleeping, lying down or sitting doing nothing!

Jungle cats

47 More than half of all wild cats live in forests and jungles. In some of these forests, the weather stays hot and wet all year round. In others there are long dry spells, followed by periods of heavy rain. These rainy seasons are known as monsoons. Both types of forest are packed full of animal and plant life.

▶ Jaguars live in South American rainforests, but often stray onto farmland and prey on domestic cattle.

48 Tigers hide in tall grass and thick vegetation. As the sunlight and shadows flicker on the tiger's stripy fur, it blends into the background. It moves little during the day and spends most of its time resting. As the sun fades, it creeps through the forest, its paws softly padding across the forest floor. It is looking and listening for any animal that it may catch unawares.

▲ Tigers prefer wet habitats and they are strong swimmers.

49 Leopards are skilful hunters. Despite this, they are becoming increasingly rare in rainforest areas due to the destruction of their habitat.

▶ Trees provide leopards with ideal places to observe unwary prey animals.

50 Some jungle areas are protected and people are not allowed to cut down the trees. These areas are called 'reserves' and are meant to provide a place where animals, including all kinds of big cats, can live safely in peace.

Swift and sure

51 Like smaller cats, big cats are very athletic. They are able to run, climb, pounce and leap almost silently. These are important skills when hunting, as they need to get as close to their prey as they can before attacking it.

▼ Like all cats, caracals run by pushing off with both hind legs together but land on one front foot and then the other.

▲ Large nostrils mean a cheetah can take lots of oxygen into its lungs during a sprint.

52 Cheetahs are the fastest of all cats. Their spines are so bendy they can bring their hind legs forward between their front paws when they run, allowing them to take huge steps as they bound forwards. Unlike most cats, they do not have retractable claws on their feet. When they run their claws stick into the ground like the spikes on an athlete's shoes.

QUIZ

1. Are cheetah's nostrils large or small?
2. Why do lions keep low when stalking prey?
3. Why do leopards have long tails?

Answers:
1. Large 2. To avoid being seen 3. To help them keep their balance

▼ A lion gets close to potential prey, keeping low to the grass and placing its paws carefully and silently to avoid being seen or heard.

53 Some cats, such as leopards, spend a lot of their time in trees. Long tails help them to keep their balance as they move along narrow branches. They can chase monkeys high up into a tree, keeping their footing on branches that seem too flimsy to support a squirrel!

◀ If the prey it is chasing falls out of the tree, a leopard can turn and race down headfirst to catch it.

54 Cats don't really have nine lives, although it often seems that they can survive almost any scrape they get into. Their strength and quick reactions can save their lives. When a cat falls out of a tree, it can twist its body round so that it lands on its feet – and walk away with its head held high and a flick of its tail!

American athlete

▼ Pumas live in the New World, from the southern tip of South America all the way to Alaska.

55 **The puma is a great athlete.** Pumas have long hind legs packed with muscles – ideal for jumping, running and climbing. Of all the big cats, these are the most graceful. They can spring 2 metres into a tree then bound up a further 18 metres before leaping down to the ground.

56 Pumas have many names. These include cougar, panther, red jaguar, catamount, deer tiger and mountain lion. People from Central and South America call them *chimblea*, *miztil*, *pagi* or *leopardo*.

57 When you live in a hot climate and are covered in a coat of fur, it can be difficult to keep cool. Pumas, like other cats, pant to lose heat. When an animal pants, it opens its mouth and lets its tongue hang out. This means that water can evaporate off the surface of the tongue, lowering the animal's body temperature.

58 Rabbits, mice, rats and hares are popular prey for pumas. They will also attack larger mammals, including deer, cattle and elks. In some places, humans have built houses in or near the pumas' natural habitat. This has resulted in people being attacked – even killed – by these wild animals. Now, people are beginning to realize that they have to respect the pumas' natural instincts and stay away from their territory.

60 Although pumas can kill porcupines, it is not an easy task. They need to flip the prickly creature onto its back before biting its soft belly. If the porcupine manages to spear the puma with one of its many spines, the wound may prove fatal.

I DON'T BELIEVE IT!

Pumas can't roar. Instead, they make an ear-piercing scream that scares both humans and animals alike, and gives it one of its many names: 'mountain-screamer'.

59 These big cats are highly skilled killers. They hunt by slowly creeping up on an unsuspecting victim. When ready, they pounce, knocking their prey to the ground in one sudden hit. A single, swift bite kills the puma's victim immediately.

Life in a cold climate

▼ Snow leopards wrap their long tails around their bodies when resting, to keep in heat. Females will keep themselves warm by lining their dens with their own fur.

61 There are no wild cats living in the Antarctic. Maybe the weather is too cold for them or there are too few animals to eat. Some big cats do live in cold climates though. Like other animals in these remote areas, they grow thick fur and store extra layers of fat under their skin to keep warm.

62 The beautiful snow leopard lives in one of the most challenging habitats in the world. They survive the extreme cold because they have very thick fur, especially in winter. A snow leopard's grey coat helps to camouflage it in snow. During the summer, snow leopards often take a dip in mountain streams to cool themselves down. Snow leopards live alone and travel across a huge area searching for food. They hunt yaks, asses, sheep and goats as well as smaller mammals and birds.

63 The lynx can change its coat according to the weather. Its winter coat is much more dense, with a mane-like ruff around its head and long, thick hair on its paws, which act like snow shoes. The lynx's summer coat is so different that you might not think it was the same animal! This cat lives in pine forests across northern Europe and Asia.

▲ Female lynxes usually give birth to one to four kittens, in a den sheltered from the harsh temperatures.

▲ Siberian tigers hunt other creatures that can survive in their harsh climate, such as wild boar, moose, sika deer and bears.

I DON'T BELIEVE IT!

While Siberian tigers survive winters at temperatures as low as −33°C, Bengal tigers try to keep cool in hot forests where temperatures can reach a sweltering 38°C!

64 Siberian tigers live in cold climates in Russia and China. Their coats are paler with brown stripes, rather than the more common black stripes. During the winter months their fur grows long, thick and shaggy to help keep them warm.

Super senses

65 At night, cats can see four times better than humans. This is because they have a layer at the back of the eye that reflects light. This helps cats to see things clearly in low light.

▶ Cats have eyes on the front of their heads. Eyes in this position are best placed for judging distance. This leopard has fantastic night vision but its colour vision is not as good as ours.

66 All cats have flexible ears that they can turn towards any sounds they hear. Cats also use their ears to show how they are feeling. An angry cat will lower and twist its ears so that they are lying almost flat against its head.

67 Cats sniff their food before eating to check it is not bad or poisonous. They also use their sense of smell to discover if other animals have passed by, by sniffing the bushes and trees in their territories.

①

②

KEY

1 Cats' eyes appear to glow in the dark because they have a layer of cells that reflect light.

2 Leopards use their long whiskers to help them find their way through dense jungle vegetation, especially at night.

68 A cat's whiskers are special hairs that are extra-sensitive. They are particularly useful at night when it is likely to be hunting. As the cat moves through undergrowth, its whiskers brush against the leaves, helping it choose a safe path. It is only by using all of their senses together that cats are able to move about easily in darkness.

▼ Despite their doglike appearance hyenas are more closely related to cats than dogs.

69 Cats use all of their senses to stay alive. As hunters, they need to be able to find, chase and catch their prey. Although big cats do not have many natural enemies, they need to watch out for scavengers, such as hyenas. These animals gang up on big cats and steal their meals.

A coat to die for

70 The jaguar is the owner of a beautiful fur coat – so beautiful that many people wanted to own it too. Although it is against the law to capture a jaguar for its skin, they are still hunted. Jaguars live in rainforests, often in areas where farmers are cutting back trees to grow crops. As jaguars' habitats continue to shrink, so will their numbers.

▶ Jaguars always live near water. They like swampy areas, or places that flood during wet seasons.

71 At first glance a jaguar looks like a leopard, but it is possible to tell them apart. A jaguar's head is bigger and rounder than a leopard's, with round ears not pointed ones. Its tail is quite a bit shorter than the leopard's and its shoulders are broad and packed with muscle.

72 Of all the big cats, jaguars are the most water-loving. They are strong swimmers and seem to enjoy bathing in rivers. Jaguars live in Central and South America but less than a hundred years ago, they were living as far north as California and Texas. They are the largest of South America's big cats.

73 Young jaguars climb trees where they hunt for birds and small mammals. As they grow bigger they become too heavy for the branches. Adults tend to stay on the ground, or in water, to hunt.

▲ Capybaras have webbed feet, and feed on grass and aquatic plants.

75 Jaguars hunt a wide range of animals including deer, tapirs, birds, fish and capybaras. Capybaras are the world's heaviest rodent and can measure up to 130 centimetres in length.

74 Jaguars' powerful jaws are so strong that they can crack open the hard shells of turtles and tortoises. These cats will even kill large animals, such as cattle and horses. It is their habit of killing cows that upsets many people who share the jaguars' territory. Cattle are very important to the farmers, who may poison or shoot jaguars that are killing their livestock.

▼ This jaguar has caught a caiman (a small crocodile-like creature). They are ambush killers, and often despatch their prey with a single bite.

Can you see me?

76 Patterned fur has helped cats survive, but it may be the death of them. For centuries, people have hunted cats for their beautiful coats. In some cases this has brought big cats to the edge of extinction.

▼ Thick, sun-bleached grass and shrubs provide ideal cover for tawny-coloured lion cubs.

▼ The tiger is the only cat with stripes. No two tigers have the same pattern.

77 A cat's fur keeps it warm when the weather is cold and cool when it is too hot. The fur is made up of two layers – a short and fluffy bottom layer and a top layer that is made of longer coloured fur.

78 The pattern on a cat's coat helps it to blend in with its surroundings. This is called camouflage. Spots blend in with the effect of dappled sunlight, stripes with long grasses.

▼ Jaguars are most active around dawn and dusk, when their spotted coats help them to blend into the shadows of the leaves.

Leopard

79 The spots on the coats of leopards and jaguars are called rosettes. Leopards have smaller, simpler rosettes that are grouped more closely together than those of jaguars. Can you spot the difference?

Jaguar

Supercat

80 Leopards can live close to humans but never be seen by them. They live in Africa and as far east as Malaysia, China and Korea. Leopards hunt by night and sleep in the day. They are possibly the most common of all the big cats, but are rarely seen in the wild.

▼ There are probably more leopards in the wild than all the other big cats put together. This success has earned leopards the nickname 'supercat'.

81 Leopards may sit in the branches of a tree, waiting patiently for their meal to come to them. As their prey strolls past, the leopard drops from the branches and silently, quickly, kills its victim.

82 Leopards nearly always hunt at night. A leopard approaches its prey in absolute silence, making sure that it does not snap a twig or rustle leaves. With incredible control, it places its hind paws onto the exact places where its forepaws had safely rested. When it is within striking distance of its victim it will attack.

83 Leopards are not fussy eaters. They will eat dung beetles, frogs or birds if nothing better comes along. They prefer to hunt monkeys, pigs and antelopes.

84 Once a leopard has caught its meal, it does not want to lose it to passing scavengers such as hyenas or jackals. The leopard might climb up a tree, hauling its prey with it. It may choose to eat immediately or store the animal for later. Hiding food like this is called 'caching' (say 'cashing').

▼ Leopards have very strong front legs, so they can haul large prey into the safety of a tree's branches.

85 The name 'panther' is usually given to pumas, but it is also used for leopards that have black fur. Black panthers are not a different type of leopard – some cubs are simply born with black fur rather than the normal tawny-brown hide.

▼ Get close enough to a black panther and you'll see that its fur is spotted.

Scaredy cat

86 The world's most mysterious cat is the clouded leopard. It is very shy and very rare. In fact, it is difficult to say how many of these pretty creatures are alive today, it is so unusual to even spot one! It is about 2 metres in length, half of which is its tail, which it uses to help balance in the trees.

87 Clouded leopards are excellent climbers and live in the forests of Southeast Asia, from Nepal to southern China. As it was once believed that they spent most of their time in trees, they were given the name 'tree cats' in Malaysia. Scientists studying them now think that they also live in grassland and mangrove swamps, and spend at least as much time on the ground as they do in the trees. Clouded leopards eat wild boar, monkeys and deer, which they catch by stalking.

88 The clouded leopard is a big cat that behaves like a little cat! It can jump around in trees as easily as a domestic tabby. These agile animals have been seen running headfirst down a tree trunk and even hanging upside-down by their hind feet. If that isn't enough, these gymnasts like swimming too!

89 No one knows how many clouded leopards are left in the wild, but experts agree their numbers are declining. This is partly because their habitat is being destroyed, but they are also hunted for their fur. Their teeth and bones are used in Asian 'traditional medicines'. Sadly, clouded leopards do not live happily in zoos either, rarely breeding in captivity.

◄ Little is known about clouded leopards. They sleep all day and only hunt at night. Despite their length, these cats weigh only about 20 kilograms – roughly the same as a six-year-old child.

I DON'T BELIEVE IT!

Clouded leopards can leap distances of more than 5 metres as they clamber through the treetops of their forest home.

Cat cousins

90 Several types of small wild cat live around the world. There are about 37 types, or species, of cat – big and small. Added to this there are 300 breeds of domestic (pet) cat. Whether they are big or small, all cats are natural-born predators.

91 The serval is one of the world's bounciest cats. It can leap one metre high and travel a distance of 4 metres as it jumps like a jack-in-the-box to strike at its prey. All this effort may be for a small supper of frogs or locusts, which are some of the serval's favourite titbits.

▼ The African serval often hunts water voles in the reeds and rushes that surround lakes and waterholes.

92 The serval is unusual because it hunts during the day. Most cats prefer to hunt at night or during the dimly-lit hours of morning or evening. Servals live in the African savannah and look very similar to cheetahs, with a slim, graceful body and long, slender forelimbs.

93
Like its neighbour, the jaguar, the ocelot has been hunted for its fur. It lives in the forests, grasslands and swamps of South America. Ocelots usually live alone or in pairs and will eat almost anything they can catch. Extremely agile, an ocelot can leap from the ground on a dark night and grab a low-flying bat in its paws or mouth.

▲ Until the hunting of these extraordinary cats was made illegal, as many as 200,000 ocelot pelts (skins) were sold every year.

94
A Eurasian lynx can kill animals four times bigger than itself. Its back legs are slightly longer than its front legs, providing it with extra power to pounce on prey in one swift bound. It is one of the biggest predators in Europe – only the brown bear and grey wolf are bigger.

◀ Like all lynxes, the Eurasian lynx has a short tail and long tufts of fur on the tip of each ear.

95
One super-springy cat is the caracal. It can leap 3 metres into the air to swipe at a passing bird. A long time ago, this fine hunter was trained to catch birds and hares in India and Iran. Caracals live in dry, scrubby habitats, so it's also known as the desert lynx.

▼ Caracals are incredible athletes, relying on speed to chase down prey, from hares to small antelopes.

A race against time

96 Most of the cats featured in this book are threatened with extinction. That means that they could disappear completely from the wild in the near future. One of the main reasons for this is the destruction of their habitat. All over the world, people and animals are fighting for space. Predators need space to hunt, but people need land to grow crops and graze cattle. Large areas of forest are also cut down to sell the trees or look for valuable minerals underground.

▼ When rainforests are cut down, millions of animals lose their homes.

I DON'T BELIEVE IT!
Closely related to the African lion, the Asiatic lion was hunted almost to extinction in the 19th century. Only about 300 are left in the wild, and they are now protected.

97 It is the misfortune of many big cats that they have wonderful fur. For the last few hundred years, cats have been killed in their hundreds of thousands so that people can wear their skins. Most of this hunting is now against the law, but it still continues. Farmers also kill big cats that steal their cattle and other animals. These people need their animals to feed their families, or to sell to make money.

▲ The beautiful Iberian lynx mostly eats rabbits, deer and ducks. Cubs are usually born in April and stay with their mother until the following spring.

98 Wherever possible, zoos and wildlife parks keep big cats safe. Scientists help the animals to breed in the hope that one day they can be returned to the wild. It is not always so simple, though. Cheetahs and clouded leopards, for example, are very difficult to breed.

99 The Iberian lynx, which only lives in Spain and Portugal, is considered the most endangered of all the larger cats. It is now fully protected by law, but its habitat is so tiny that it doesn't have much chance of survival in the wild.

100 The best way to shoot a big cat is through a camera lens. Tourists will pay a lot of money if they are promised the sight of a big cat. Now, in many places, the local people are doing everything they can to look after their wildlife so they can share it with visitors who come to their country.

◀ Not long ago, people shot lions with guns. Now tourists come to Africa to shoot close-up photographs of big cats in their natural habitat.

Index